MW01193765

Scrumptious Muffins

By: Sara Winlet

Copyright © 2012 All rights reserved
No part of this publication may be reproduced in any form or by any
means, including scanning, photocopying, or otherwise. Without prior
written permission from the copyright holder.

Visit My Other Books
Scrumptious Scones

Scrumptious Breakfast Casseroles

Scrumptious Cookies

Scrumptious Pies

Scrumptious Cupcakes

Muffins

There is nothing like waking up in the morning to a wonderful hot moist muffin. You can smell the wonderful aroma through out your home, which couldn't be more wonderful in my world. Everyone has a favorite flavor, for me its a blueberry crumb topped muffin. Why buy muffins at the bakery for three dollars each, when you can make a whole dozen for that price at home. With my Scrumptious Muffin recipe book you can save money and have hot delicious muffins anytime at home. Not only will you have great breakfast muffins, but also some savory, delectable dinner muffins as well. Also, you can top these wonderful muffins with the great butter spread recipes at the end of the book. With my recipe collection your house will have the wonderful aroma of piping hot muffins, that your family will love to wake up to.

Table of Contents

TIPS:

When baking muffins, If you coat fruit or chocolate chips with flour, they will not fall to the bottom of the muffins while baking. Also, I use melted butter (not margarine) instead of oil for all of my baking. Use an ice cream scooper for the batter to make the perfect muffin size every time. If you use muffin cups, I like to use aluminum muffin cups to help with sticking. When making a topping that calls for butter, use a cheese grater to grate cold butter into the streusel topping.

SWEET

Strawberry Patch Muffins

1 3/4 cups all-purpose flour
1/2 cup granulated sugar
1/2 cup milk
1 egg
1/4 cup melted butter
1/2 teaspoon salt
2 teaspoons baking powder
1 cup chopped strawberries

Preheat oven to 375 degrees F.

In a medium bowl, mix together melted butter, milk ,egg and set aside. In a large bowl, combine flour, salt, baking powder, and sugar. Toss in strawberries and stir to coat. Pour milk mixture into flour mixture and stir together. Fill 8 paper lined-muffin cups about 2/3 full and bake for 20-25 minutes or until middle is done and tops are lightly golden brown.

October Pumpkin Cranberry Muffins

2 1/4 cups all-purpose flour
2 eggs
1/2 cup melted butter
1 cup canned pure pumpkin
2 cups sugar
1 tablespoon pumpkin-pie spice
1 teaspoon baking soda
1/2 teaspoon salt
1 cup chopped cranberries

Preheat oven to 350 degrees F.

In medium bowl, combine eggs, sugar, melted butter, and pumpkin and mix well. In a large bowl, combine flour, spice, baking soda and salt. Pour egg mixture into flour mixture and stir until dry ingredients are moist. Fold in cranberries, then spoon batter into paper-lined muffin cups to about 2/3 full. Bake for 20-25 minutes or until center is done and tops are lightly golden brown.

Berry Raspberry Muffins

2 cups all-purpose flour
1 egg
3 teaspoon baking powder
1/2 cup sugar
1/2 teaspoon salt
3/4 cup milk
1/3 cup melted butter
1/2 teaspoon nutmeg
1 teaspoon vanilla
2 cups fresh or frozen raspberries (keep frozen)
1 teaspoon lemon zest

Preheat oven to 400 degrees F.

In a medium bowl, combine flour, sugar, baking powder, salt and lemon zest. Mix together, add raspberries to flour mixture and coat well. In a medium bowl, mix together milk, melted butter, vanilla, and egg, add to flour mixture and gently mix. Fill 12 paper lined-muffin cups 2/3 full with batter. Bake for 15-20 minutes until center is done and tops are lightly golden brown.

Fresh Fig Muffins

2 cups all-purpose flour plus 2 tablespoons flour
1/3 cup sugar
4 large fresh figs chopped
1 tablespoon baking powder
1 cup milk
1 egg beaten
1/2 teaspoon salt
1/4 cup melted butter

Preheat oven to 350 degrees F.

Coat fig pieces in 2 tablespoons of flour, and set aside. In a large bowl, mix flour, sugar, baking powder, and salt then set aside. In a small bowl, mix milk, egg, and butter. Mix milk mixture with flour mixture until dry ingredients are moist, then fold in figs. Spoon batter into paper-lined muffin cups to about 2/3 full. Bake for 20-25 minutes until center is done and tops are lightly golden brown.

Heavenly Chocolate Chip Muffins

2 cups all-purpose flour
1/3 cup sugar
2 tablespoons baking powder
1/3 cup light brown sugar packed
2/3 cups milk
1/2 teaspoon salt
1/2 cup melted butter
2 eggs beaten
1 teaspoon vanilla
12 oz package chocolate chips

Preheat oven to 400 degrees F.

In a large bowl, mix flour, both sugars, baking powder, and salt and set aside. In a medium bowl, mix milk, eggs, butter, and vanilla. Combine milk and flour mixture until moist, then fold in chocolate chips. Spoon into paper lined-muffin cups to about 2/3 full and bake for 15-20 minutes until center is done and tops are golden brown. Sprinkle with a mixture of brown sugar and cinnamon.

Rich Chocolate Chip Banana Muffins

1 1/2 cups all-purpose flour
2/3 cups sugar
1/2 cup melted butter
1 egg
1/4 cup milk
1/4 teaspoon salt
1 1/2 teaspoon baking powder
1 cup mashed ripe bananas
3/4 cup semisweet chocolate chips

Preheat oven to 350 degrees F.

In a large bowl, mix flour, sugar, baking powder, and salt. In a small bowl, combine mashed bananas, egg, melted butter, and milk. Mix well. Stir egg mixture with dry ingredients until lightly blended. Stir in chocolate chips, then spoon batter into 12 paper lined muffin cups about 2/3 full. Bake until center is done and tops are golden brown. Sprinkle with a mixture of cinnamon and brown sugar.

Chocolate Chocolate Chip Muffins

1 2/3 cups all-purpose flour
1/2 cup sugar
1/3 cup unsalted butter
6 oz semisweet chocolate squares
3/4 cup buttermilk
1 egg beaten
1 1/2 teaspoon vanilla extract
1 teaspoon baking soda
1/2 teaspoon salt
1 cup mini semi-sweet chocolate chips

Preheat oven to 400 degrees F.

In a small saucepan, melt semi-sweet chocolate squares and butter over low heat. Let stand for 10 minutes. In a medium bowl, mix buttermilk, sugar, egg, and vanilla. Stir in cooled chocolate and butter mixture. In a large bowl mix flour, baking soda, and salt. Add in the wet ingredients and stir until just combined. Fold in mini chocolate chips then spoon batter into paper lined muffin cups to about 2/3 full. Bake for 20-25 minutes until center is done.

Berry Blueberry Lemon Muffins

1/2 cup butter
2 eggs
1 cup sugar
1/2 cup milk
2 cups all-purpose flour
2 tablespoon lemon juice
2 teaspoons lemon zest
1/2 teaspoon salt
2 teaspoons baking powder
1 teaspoon vanilla
2 cups fresh or frozen blueberries (keep frozen)
Topping:
1/4 cup brown sugar
2 tablespoon of butter

Preheat oven to 350 degrees F.

In a medium bowl, blend butter and sugar, then mix in eggs and milk. Add in flour, baking powder, salt, vanilla and lemon juice and mix all ingredients. Gently fold in blueberries, then spoon batter into lined muffin cups about 2/3 full. In a small bowl, combine brown sugar, lemon zest, and butter, crumb together and sprinkle over tops of unbaked muffins. Bake for 20-25 minutes until done in the center and lightly golden brown.

Luscious Lemon Raspberry Muffins

2 cups all-purpose flour
1/2 cup melted butter
1 cup sugar
2 eggs beaten
1 cup buttermilk
1/2 teaspoon baking powder
1/2 teaspoon salt
1 teaspoon lemon extract
1 cup fresh or frozen raspberries

Preheat oven to 400 degrees F.

In a small bowl, mix eggs, buttermilk, melted butter, and lemon extract then set aside. In a large bowl combine flour, sugar, baking powder, and salt. Add in milk mixture and stir until moistened. Gently fold in raspberries and spoon into paper lined muffin cups until about 2/3 full. Bake for 20-25 minutes until center is done and tops are lightly golden brown.

Almond Cherry Muffins

2 cups all-purpose flour
1 tablespoon baking powder
1/2 teaspoon salt
1/2 cup sugar
1 large eggs
1 cup milk
1/4 cup melted butter
3/4 teaspoon ground cinnamon
1 cup chopped fresh or frozen cherries (pitted)
1/2 teaspoon almond extract
1/2 cup chopped almonds

Preheat oven to 375 degrees F.

In a medium bowl, combine flour, sugar, salt, baking powder, and cinnamon. Add cherries and stir gently. In a small bowl, mix egg, milk, melted butter, and almond extract. Add milk mixture into dry ingredients and stir until moistened. Spoon batter into paper lined muffin cups about 2/3 full. Sprinkle with Chopped almonds. Bake for 20-25 minutes until done in the center.

Wild Blackberry Muffins

2 cups all-purpose flour
2 teaspoons baking powder
1/2 teaspoon salt
1/2 cup milk
1/2 cup softened butter
1 1/4 cups sugar plus 1 tablespoon divided
2 eggs
2 cups fresh wild blackberries

Preheat oven to 375 degrees F.

In a large bowl, blend butter and 1 ¼ cup sugar, add eggs one at a time and beat well. In a medium bowl combine flour, baking powder, and salt. Alternate flour mixture and milk into butter, beating well after each addition. Gently fold in blackberries. Spoon batter into paper-lined muffin cups about 2/3 full. Sprinkle with reserved 1 tablespoon of sugar. Bake for 20-25 minutes or until center is done and tops are golden brown.

Harvest Cinnamon Apple Muffins

1 1/2 cups all-purpose flour
3/4 cup sugar
2 teaspoon salt
2 teaspoons baking powder
1/3 cup melted butter
1 teaspoon cinnamon
1 egg
1/3 cup milk
2 tart apples (diced)

Topping:
1/2 cup cold butter
1/3 cup all-purpose flour
1/2 cup granulated sugar
1 1/2 teaspoon ground cinnamon

Preheat oven to 400 degrees F.

In a large bowl combine flour, sugar, salt, baking powder, and 1 teaspoon cinnamon. Add egg, melted butter, and milk to flour mixture and mix only until moistened. Fold apples into batter, then spoon into paper-lined muffin cups about 2/3 full. In a small bowl mix together topping ingredients with a fork until it resembles crumbs. Sprinkle over unbaked muffins then bake for 20-25 minutes or until center is done.

Ripe Banana Muffins

1 1/2 cups all-purpose flour
3/4 cup granulated sugar
1 teaspoon baking soda
1 teaspoon baking powder
1/2 teaspoon salt
1 egg
1 1/2 cups mashed ripe bananas
1/3 cup melted butter

Topping:
2 tablespoon all-purpose flour
1/4 teaspoon cinnamon
1/3 cup brown sugar
1 tablespoon cold butter

Preheat oven to 375 degrees F.

In a large bowl, combine flour, baking soda, baking powder, and salt then set aside. In a medium bowl, mix together bananas, sugar, egg, and melted butter. Stir banana mixture into flour mixture until moistened. Spoon batter into paper-lined muffin cups about 2/3 full. In a small bowl mix topping ingredients with a fork, then sprinkle over tops of muffins. Bake for 20-25 minutes or until middle is done and tops are golden brown.

Very Berry Cranberry Muffins

1/2 cup granulated sugar
2 cups all-purpose flour
1/2 cup softened butter
2 eggs
1 teaspoon vanilla extract
1 cup sour cream
1 teaspoon baking powder
1/2 teaspoon baking soda
1/2 teaspoon ground nutmeg
1/4 teaspoon salt
1 cup chopped fresh or frozen cranberries
Topping:
2 tablespoons sugar
1/8 teaspoon ground nutmeg

Preheat oven to 400 degrees F.

In a large bowl, mix butter and sugar. Add eggs and vanilla and mix well. Fold in sour cream then set aside. In a medium bowl, combine flour, baking powder, baking soda, nutmeg, and salt. Add flour mixture into butter mixture and mix only until just moistened. Fold in cranberries and spoon into paper-lined muffin cups about 2/3 full. In a small bowl, combine topping ingredients and sprinkle over tops of muffins. Bake for 20-25 minutes or until center is done and tops are golden brown.

Peaches and Cream Muffins

2 1/4 cups all-purpose flour
2 tablespoons sugar
2 teaspoons baking powder
1 teaspoon baking soda
1/4 cup butter
3 cups canned peaches (drained and diced)
1/3 cup sour cream
1 egg (beaten)

Preheat oven to 400 degrees F.

In a medium bowl, combine flour, sugar, baking powder and baking soda then cut in cold butter until mixture resembles coarse crumbs set aside. In a medium bowl, combine 1/3 cup sour cream, egg and diced peaches. Add to flour mixture and mix until moistened. Spoon into paper-lined muffin cups until about 2/3 full. Bake for 15 minutes or until center is done and tops are golden brown.

Sour Cherry Lemon Muffins

1 (16 oz) can of pitted sour cherries
2 cups all-purpose flour
3 teaspoon baking powder
1/2 cup sugar
1/4 teaspoon salt
1 egg
3/4 cup milk
1 tablespoon lemon juice
1/4 cup melted butter
1 tablespoon lemon zest

Preheat oven to 375 degrees F.

In a large bowl, combine flour, sugar, baking powder, and salt set aside. In a medium bowl, beat egg and milk. Add to flour mixture and combine until just moistened. Stir in lemon zest, lemon juice and melted butter, and fold in cherries. Spoon into paper-lined muffin cups until about 2/3 full and bake for 25-30 minutes or until center is done and tops are golden brown.

SAVORY

Cowboy Southwestern Dinner Muffins

2 cups all-purpose flour
1/4 cup sugar
10 strips of bacon
1 tablespoon baking powder
3/4 cup milk
1 egg
1 1/2 cups shredded cheddar cheese
1/4 cup diced green chilies

Preheat oven to 400 degrees F.

In a medium skillet, cook bacon until crisp, reserving 1/3 cup drippings. Crumble and set aside. In a large bowl, combine flour, sugar, baking powder then set aside. In a medium bowl, whisk egg, milk and bacon drippings. Add egg mixture to flour mixture and combine until just moistened. Fold in cheese, chilies and bacon. Spoon batter into buttered muffin pan or foil lined muffin cups until 2/3 full. Bake for 15-20 minutes or until center is done and tops are golden brown.

Cheddar Cheese Bacon Muffins

2 cups all-purpose flour
1 cup shredded cheddar cheese
8 strips bacon (cooked, and crumbled)
2 tablespoons sugar
3 teaspoon baking powder
1/8 teaspoon garlic powder
1 egg
1/4 teaspoon salt
1 cup milk
1/4 cup melted butter

Preheat oven to 400 degrees F.

In a large bowl, combine flour, sugar, baking powder, garlic powder, salt, cheese and bacon then set aside. In a small bowl, whisk egg, milk and melted butter. Add to flour mixture and combine until just moistened. Spoon batter into buttered muffin cups or foil lined muffin cups until about 2/3 full. Bake for 15 to 20 minutes until center is done and tops are golden brown.

Cheddar Cheese Dill Muffins

3 1/2 cups all-purpose flour
1 cup shredded cheddar cheese
3 tablespoons sugar
2 tablespoons baking powder
2 teaspoons dill weed
1 teaspoon salt
1 3/4 cups milk
2 eggs lightly beaten
1/4 cup melted butter

Preheat oven to 400 degrees F.

In a medium bowl, combine flour, cheese, sugar, baking powder, dill, and salt, then set aside. In a medium bowl, whisk milk, eggs, and melted butter then add to flour mixture and combine until just moistened. Spoon batter into buttered muffin pan or foil lined muffin cups until about 2/3 full. Bake for 25-30 minutes or until center is done and tops are golden brown.

Sausage Cheddar Muffins

1 (16 oz.) package breakfast sausage
2 cups Bisquick
1 1/2 cups shredded cheddar cheese
3 eggs
1 cup cornmeal
1 3/4 cups milk

Preheat oven to 375 degrees F.

In a medium, skillet brown sausage until no longer pink, drain and set aside. In a medium bowl, mix cornmeal, Bisquick, milk and eggs. Add in cheese and sausage and mix well. Spoon batter into buttered muffin pan or foil lined muffin cups until about 2/3 full. Bake for 15 minutes or until center is done and tops are golden brown.

SWEET BUTTER SPREADS

Sweet Honey Butter

1/2 cup butter (softened)
1/2 cup honey
2 teaspoons lemon juice

Place all ingredients into a medium mixing bowl, whip on high for about 1 minute or until light and fluffy.

Harvest Pumpkin Honey Butter

1/2 cup softened butter
1/2 cup honey
3 tablespoons canned pure pumpkin
1 teaspoon pumpkin pie spice

In a small bowl, mix honey, pumpkin, and pumpkin pie spice then set aside. In a medium mixing bowl, whip butter until fluffy about 1 minute. Add honey mixture to butter and mix on high until mixture is fluffy and smooth. Chill butter several hours or overnight for flavors to blend.

Berry Cranberry Butter

1 cup unsalted butter (softened)
6 tablespoons powder sugar
2 teaspoons lemon zest
3/4 cups cranberries

Place cranberries with powder sugar in a food processor and pulse until coarsely chopped, then add butter and blend until chunky. Place in refrigerator until ready to use.

Strawberry Patch Butter

1 cup butter (softened)
3/4 cup frozen strawberries (thawed and drained)
3 tablespoons powdered sugar

Mix all ingredients in a blender until smooth. Refrigerate butter until ready to use.

Honey Pecan Butter

1/2 cup butter
1/2 cup churned honey
1/3 cup toasted chopped pecans

Place butter and honey in medium mixing bowl and whip until smooth. Place pecans on a cookie sheet and bake at 300 degrees for about 7 minutes or until slightly roasted. Fold chopped pecans into butter mixture.

Cinnamon Cream Cheese Butter

½ cup butter
2 tablespoons cream cheese
¼ cup powder sugar
2 teaspoons cinnamon

Place all ingredients in a medium mixing bowl and whip on high for about 1 minute or until light and fluffy.

Orange Coconut Honey Butter

1/2 cup butter (softened)
2 tablespoons honey
1 tablespoon orange zest
1 tablespoon finely flaked coconut

Place all ingredients in a medium mixing bowl, whip on high for about
1 minute or until light and fluffy.

SAVORY BUTTER SPREADS

Rosemary Marjoram Butter

1/4 cup butter (softened)
1/2 teaspoon dried rosemary
1/4 teaspoon dried marjoram (crushed)

In a medium mixing bowl, whip butter until light and fluffy. Add rosemary and marjoram mix until well combined.

Garlic Dill Cream Cheese Butter

1/2 cup butter
1/2 cup cream cheese
1 garlic clove (finely minced)
1 tablespoon fresh parsley (finely minced)
2 tablespoons fresh dill (finely minced)

In a medium mixing bowl, combine all ingredients and whip until light and fluffy.

Lemon and Herb Butter

1/2 cup butter
1 tablespoon lemon zest
1/4 cup fresh parsley (finely chopped)
1 teaspoon basil
1 teaspoon oregano

In a medium mixing bowl, whip all ingredients together until light and fluffy.

Cheddar Garlic Butter

1/2 cup butter (softened)
1 cup shredded cheddar cheese
1/2 teaspoon worcestershire sauce
1/4 teaspoon garlic salt

In a medium mixing bowl, combine all ingredients and whip until light and fluffy.

John 3:16 For God so loved the world, that he gave his only begotten Son, that whosoever believeth in him should not perish, but have everlasting life.

43559699R00026

Made in the USA
San Bernardino, CA
20 December 2016